GW01459054

RYA

National Sailing Scheme

Syllabus & Logbook

© RYA

Fifth Edition 2022

Reprinted June 2023, January 2024, January 2025

The Royal Yachting Association

RYA House, Ensign Way,

Hamble, Southampton,

Hampshire SO31 4YA

Tel: 02380 604 100

Web: www.rya.org.uk

We welcome feedback on our publications at publications@rya.org.uk

You can check content updates for RYA publications at
www.rya.org.uk/go/bookschangelog

ISBN 978-1-910017388

RYA Order Code G4

Cover design: Jude Williams

Photographic credits: Ian Aldridge (Minorca Sailing), Nick Dempsey,
Laura Eaves (Sweet Bay Photography), Paddy James (RS Sailing), James Tomlinson,
Paul Wyeth, Nic Wymer

Typeset: Jude Williams

Proofreading: Matthew Gale

Printed in the UK

CONTENTS

Photo credit: Nic Wymer

INTRODUCTION

Sailing is a fantastic and diverse sport, with activities to suit everyone. The RYA National Sailing Scheme has been designed to help you enjoy whichever aspect of the sport appeals to you. All the courses in the Scheme can be taken in a dinghy, keelboat, or multihull so you can have tuition in whatever type of boat you wish.

Good sailing!

Liz McMaster
RYA Chief Instructor, Dinghy, Wing & Windsurfing

THE RYA NATIONAL SAILING SCHEME MODEL

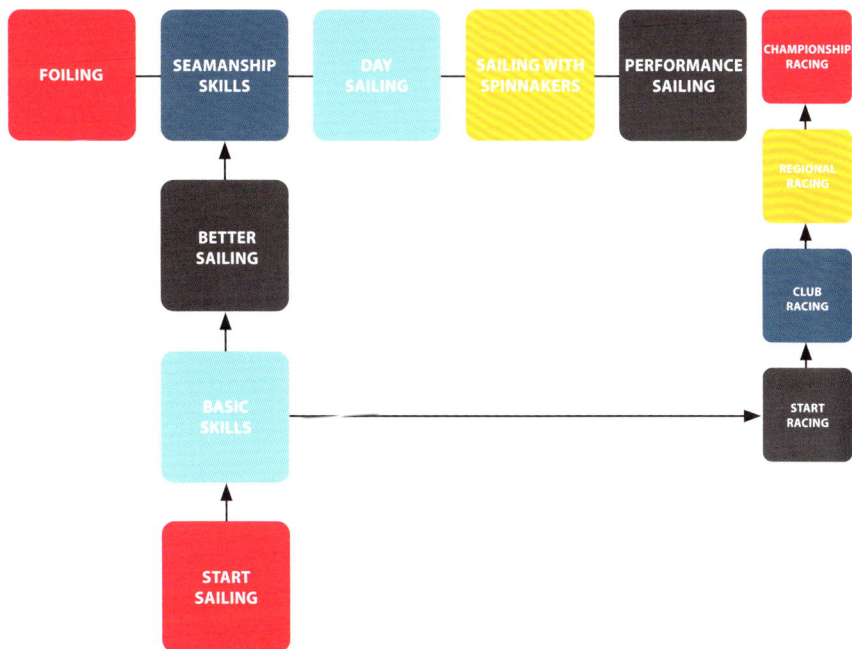

FOILING	SEAMANSHIP SKILLS	DAY SAILING	SAILING WITH SPINNAKERS	PERFORMANCE SAILING	CHAMPIONSHIP RACING

```
FOILING  ← SEAMANSHIP SKILLS → DAY SAILING → SAILING WITH SPINNAKERS → PERFORMANCE SAILING        CHAMPIONSHIP RACING
                  ↑                                                                                          ↑
              BETTER SAILING                                                                          REGIONAL RACING
                  ↑                                                                                          ↑
              BASIC SKILLS  ─────────────────────────────────────────────────────────→ START RACING → CLUB RACING
                  ↑
              START SAILING
```

THE RYA NATIONAL SAILING SCHEME

How to Find the Right Sailing Course

The reputation of the RYA National Sailing Scheme has been built on high standards and good tuition. RYA Training Centres vary according to the sailing area available and the type of boats and level of tuition on offer. Whether you wish to learn to sail locally or improve your sailing on holiday, there should be an RYA Training Centre to suit you. To select a course that will meet your needs, visit the RYA website (www.rya.org.uk/wheresmynearest) for a list of sailing schools near you.

Some RYA Training Centres have specialised facilities (including boats) for people with disabilities. Others can offer integrated courses in standard boats. Some students with disabilities may need additional help to complete the full requirements for an RYA certificate.

There is provision within the Scheme for certificates to be endorsed as appropriate. Please contact the Principal of your selected RYA Training Centre or the RYA for more information.

What is an RYA Recognised Training Centre?

Safety is a priority for the RYA. Each RYA Training Centre is regularly inspected for standards of tuition, facilities, and equipment, as laid down by RYA Training and published in the guidance notes. All must have qualified staff, suitable boats, and adequate safety cover. RYA Training Centres should display a Certificate of Recognition specifying the activities for which they are recognised. They are also required to carry public liability insurance.

For Beginners' courses run in single-handed dinghies, there should be an Instructor to a maximum of six students in single-handed dinghies, or one to three in crewed dinghies with the Instructor on board. Keelboat courses can be run with an Instructor/student ratio of up to one to four.

All training, whether inland or coastal, should cover and include tidal material relevant to the level.

At the end of your course, the Principal or Chief Instructor will decide whether certificates are to be awarded. Certificates are specific to the type of boat used, i.e. dinghy, keelboat, or multihull. If the Principal decides that further practice is necessary before awarding you a certificate, they will explain the reasons to you. Should you feel it necessary to appeal against the outcome, contact RYA Training for guidance.

The Courses

All the courses in the RYA National Sailing Scheme can be spread over a series of sessions covering a period of 16 hours or in just two days. Most are flexible and often available as evening or half-day sessions too.

Direct Assessments

Experienced sailors may wish to have direct assessment of their skills rather than taking part in a training course. The criteria are outlined in this book. Individual items will be signed off by the assessing Instructor and the declaration signed by the Principal or Chief Instructor.

Photo credit: Nic Wymer

What Next?

After taking your course you may consider joining a club, or buying a boat and joining the class association, who organise a variety of events. The RYA website (www.rya.org.uk) is a good place to find a club or locate your class association.

How to Become an Instructor

Having learnt to sail, you may enjoy passing your skills on to others. The RYA Instructor is an experienced sailor who has successfully completed a sailing test (the pre-entry test) and an Instructor training course. Further information is on the RYA website and pages 38–39. RYA Instructors should also hold a first aid certificate and the RYA Powerboat Level 2 Certificate. Full details are contained in RYA publication G14, RYA National Sailing Scheme Instructor Handbook.

Courses for Young People

The RYA also offers a training scheme for young people, the Youth Sailing Scheme. Full details are published in RYA book G11. Following completion of the Youth Sailing Scheme, young people may participate in further training through the advanced modules of the National Sailing Scheme.

Windsurfing, Powerboating, Sail and Power Cruising

The RYA organises similar training schemes for all these activities. Full details are available from the website or the RYA Training Department.

Learning Resources

The RYA produces a wide range of materials to help you learn, from handbooks to online courses. These can be obtained through RYA Training Centres and the RYA website.

Photo credit: Nic Wymer

THE DUKE OF EDINBURGH'S AWARD

Are you aged between 14 and 24 and fancy challenging yourself?

The RYA is recognised as a National Operating Authority for The Duke of Edinburgh's Award (DofE). The DofE is a voluntary, non-competitive programme of activities for anyone aged 14 to 24, providing a fantastic opportunity to experience new activities or develop existing skills.

There are three progressive levels of programmes that, when successfully completed, lead to a Bronze, Silver, or Gold Award.

Sailing as part of your DofE

Achieving a DofE Award can be made an adventure from beginning to end. Within an RYA club or training centre there are already many activities you could take part in that can count towards your DofE. These could range from:

Volunteering

Helping out at your local training centre, club, or BYS Recognised Windsurfing Club on a regular basis. This could be as an assistant, in the kitchen, or maybe even on the committee!

Physical

Regularly taking part in sailing or windsurfing activity? Why not set yourself a goal to gain a certain certificate in the RYA National Sailing or Windsurfing Schemes, or maybe participate in regular club racing?

Skill

Develop your skills, whether practical, social, or personal. You may choose to sharpen up your powerboating, learn a new skill such as boat repair work, become an Instructor, or perhaps increase your theory knowledge and learn all about meteorology!

Residential and Expedition

You may never have been away from home before, let alone used your board or boat to go on an exciting adventure with friends, so now is the time!

Further information can be found, explaining the opportunities available, on the DofE website (www.dofe.org), and the RYA website (www.rya.org.uk/training/under-16s/the-duke-of-edinburgh-award).

LEVEL 1 – START SAILING

This course provides a short introduction to sailing for novices. By the end of the course you will have a basic understanding of dinghy-handling techniques and background knowledge. It is recommended that all participants consolidate this short introduction with the Basic Skills and Better Sailing courses.

Duration: Approximately 16 hours (either spread over a series of sessions or two full days).

Practical

Has a practical understanding of:

RIGGING

Basic rigging, parts of the sail, sail controls and foils ☑

Has wind awareness ashore ☑

SAILING TECHNIQUES AND MANOEUVRES

Wind awareness afloat ☑

Reaching – sailing across the wind ☑

Stopping – lying-to ☑

Controlling speed ☑

Getting out of irons ☑

Tacking – turning the front of the boat through the wind ☑

Sailing upwind ☑

The Five Essentials ☑

Sailing downwind ☑

Gybing – turning the back of the boat through the wind, from a training run ☑

The importance of good communication when manoeuvring (double-handers) ☑

Can perform a basic capsize recovery, and understands the importance of staying with the boat* (Optional) ☐

LAUNCHING AND RECOVERY*

Can:

Secure a boat on the trolley (where location allows) ☐

Understands the principles of:

Wheeling a trolley clear of other boats and overhead cables (where location allows) ☐

Launching and leaving the shore ☑

Coming ashore and recovery of a boat ☑

ROPEWORK

Can tie a figure of eight knot, round turn and two half hitches, and secure a rope to a cleat ☑

*Not necessarily applicable to keelboats

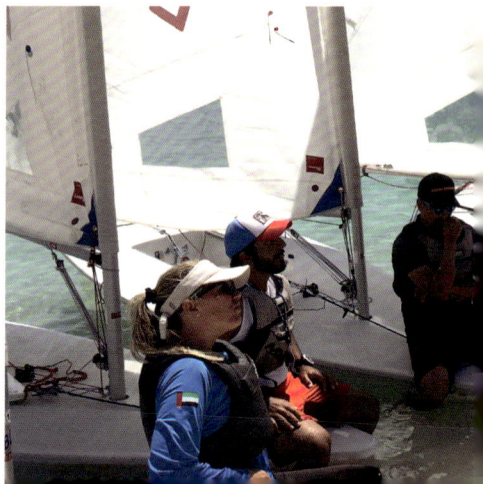

Sailing Theory

Has theoretical understanding of:

CLOTHING AND EQUIPMENT

Knows the importance of personal safety, clothing, and buoyancy ☑

SAILING BACKGROUND

Understands the 7 Common Senses (see inside front cover), such as the following areas:

An awareness of other water users ☑

Basic rules of the road – avoid a collision at all costs, power/sail, port/starboard, overtaking boat, windward boat ☑

Visual methods of attracting attention ☑

METEOROLOGY

Has an awareness of onshore and offshore winds ☑

Sources of weather information and their relevance:

Effects on sailing location ☑

Beaufort Scale ☑

Conditions appropriate to ability and sailing location ☑

Keelboat Sailors

CLOTHING AND EQUIPMENT

Understands:

Use of, and correct fitting of lifejackets ☑

Use of a safety harness if fitted ☑

MAN OVERBOARD RECOVERY

Understands:

Actions to be taken to recover a man overboard ☑

Use of mooring lines ☑

EMERGENCY EQUIPMENT AND PRECAUTIONS

Has knowledge and awareness of:

Potential hazards and risks of on-board fuel ☑

Stowage and use of fire extinguishers ☑

OTHER ASPECTS

Basic Skills Course ☑

[signature]

Chief Instructor's/~~Principal's~~ Signature

Sussex Yacht Club

RYA Training Centre

Photo credit: Nic Wymer

LEVEL 2 – BASIC SKILLS

On completion of this course, you will have a basic knowledge of sailing and sailing in light winds without an instructor on board. It will be assumed that every student starting this course has already mastered the practical skills and absorbed the background knowledge required for Start Sailing. Both courses can be combined. Dinghy or multihull capsize recovery will be conducted in a controlled manner, one boat at a time, with a suitable rescue boat in attendance.

Duration: Approximately 16 hours (either spread over a series of sessions or two full days).

Practical

Has a practical understanding of:

RIGGING

How to rig according to weather conditions ☐

Reefing ashore* ☐

SAILING TECHNIQUES AND MANOEUVRES

Leaving and returning to a beach, jetty, or mooring ☐

Coming alongside a moored boat ☐

Sailing in close company ☐

Performing a man-overboard recovery ☐

Is aware of lee-shore dangers ☐

The Five Essentials ☐

Can tack while sailing upwind, showing refined skill, losing minimal ground ☐

Can gybe in a controlled manner while sailing downwind ☐

Shows good communication when manoeuvring (double-handers) ☐

Understands and shows awareness of other water users ☐

Can sail around a short course using all points of sail and crewing skills ☐

ROPEWORK

Can tie a bowline, clove hitch, and reef knot ☐

CAPSIZE RECOVERY

Can right a capsized boat using one method of righting, and has knowledge of at least one other ☐

RACING

Understands the course and starting procedure (may be covered as onshore teaching) ☐

BASIC ADVICE FOR INDEPENDENT SAILING:

Self-reliance and basic equipment ☐

Visual methods of attracting attention ☐

Has knowledge of:

The points of sailing and the 'No-go Zone' ☐

How a sail works ☐

How a sailing boat moves (basic theory) ☐

*Not necessarily applicable to keelboats

METEOROLOGY

Has knowledge of:

Sources of relevant weather, inshore forecasts, and their interpretation ☐

The Beaufort Wind Scale ☐

When to reef ☐

How to understand a simple synoptic chart ☐

SAILING THEORY

Has theoretical understanding of:

CLOTHING AND EQUIPMENT

Knows the importance of personal safety, clothing, basic personal and boat buoyancy ☐

LAUNCHING AND RECOVERY

Boat storage ashore, launching, and recovery ☐

SAILING BACKGROUND

Has knowledge of:

Basic rules of the road – avoid collisions at all costs, power/sail, port/starboard, windward boat, overtaking boat ☐

Understands:

How to apply weather forecasts in coastal waters ☐

Tide tables, tidal sequence of springs and neaps, ebb and flow ☐

Speed over ground with/against tidal flow ☐

The effect of wind direction and tidal flow on sailing conditions ☐

The importance of informing someone ashore, and the dangers of sailing alone ☐

How to access local information and advice for sea sailing ☐

Keelboat Sailors

RIGGING

Can reef afloat ☐

ROPEWORK

Can use winches ☐

USE OF ENGINES (IF FITTED)

Has knowledge of engine checks, starting, stopping, and running procedures ☐

Can come alongside and pick up a mooring ☐

SAILING TECHNIQUES AND MANOEUVRES

Can:

Anchor ☐

Sail using transits ☐

EMERGENCY EQUIPMENT AND PRECAUTIONS

Knows the importance of first aid kits and flares, including stowage ☐

Multihull Sailors

SAILING TECHNIQUES AND MANOEUVRES

Understands the basic principles of crew weight, airflow, technique (CAT) ☐

OTHER ASPECTS

Better Sailing Course ☐

Opportunities for regular activity (local club and centre activity and groups, etc.) ☐

Purchasing your own equipment ☐

Basic racing ☐

Chief Instructor's/Principal's Signature

RYA Training Centre

LEVEL 3 – BETTER SAILING

This improver course seeks to bridge the gap between Start Sailing, Basic Skills, and the Advanced modules by offering an introduction to the different modules, allowing sailors to select more easily their preferred route within the sport. Better Sailing allows for opportunity to practise and consolidate sailing techniques, and experience some of the activities the Advanced modules have to offer, helping to build confidence and support development of good technique and independent sailing.

Additional module options are non-compulsory for completion of the Better Sailing course, but are designed to provide an introduction to the various aspects of sailing. Which elements are chosen should be discussed by student and Instructor. Where practicable, students should be provided with the opportunity to sail different dinghies during the course, single and double-handers.

Duration: Approximately 16 hours (either spread over a series of sessions or two full days).

Practical

Has a practical understanding of:

SAILING TECHNIQUES AND MANOEUVRES

Understands how to use rig and sail controls to prepare the boat according to different weather conditions and sea states ☐

Can check a spinnaker is rigged correctly (if fitted) ☐

CORE SKILLS

Can:

Leave and return to a shore, jetty, or mooring (including windward and leeward shore in light conditions) ☐

Recover a man overboard effectively ☐

Use the sail tell-tales effectively ☐

Reef a sail when required ☐

Demonstrate a 'dry capsize' ☐

Understand how to avoid inversion ☐

Sail using efficient and skilful application of the Five Essentials ☐

Tack – maintaining boat speed and balance, upwind ☐

Gybe – maintaining boat speed and balance ☐

Show good use of crew and to best effect (where applicable) ☐

Understand when, and the importance of, timing manoeuvres ☐

Sailing Background

Has theoretical understanding of:

The IRPCS, and can apply them to:

Other sailing vessels ☐

Power-driven vessels ☐

Following or crossing narrow channels ☐

Action by stand-on vessel ☐

Basic sail-control knowledge to change the sail shape and power ☐

Understands:

The points of sailing ☐

The Five Essentials ☐

Basic meteorology terminology, including the Beaufort Scale ☐

How to obtain a weather forecast ☐

How to interpret a basic synoptic chart ☐

Awareness of changing weather conditions ☐

Additional Module Options:

Has both practical and theoretical understanding of the following:

SEAMANSHIP SKILLS

Can demonstrate anchoring in various conditions ☐

Introduction to sailing in adverse conditions (centreboardless, rudderless sailing) ☐

RACE SKILLS

Has knowledge of the 'simplified World Sailing Racing Rules of Sailing' ☐

Can:

Start and finish a simple race ☐

Choose the best route to sail around a course, depending on conditions (using the Five Essentials) ☐

DAY SAILING SKILLS

Basic chart orientation – including cardinal and lateral buoyage systems ☐

Can take bearings and measure distances on a chart ☐

Understands the effect of tide and wind direction on sailing conditions ☐

Can:

Use a local tide table ☐

Follow a pre-planned route ☐

SPINNAKER SAILING SKILLS

Basic introduction to spinnaker handling as crew or helm, including rig, hoist, and drop ☐

PERFORMANCE SAILING SKILLS

Basic introduction to trapezing with Instructor on the helm (Optional – boat-dependent) ☐

Introduction to better hiking technique ☐

OTHER ASPECTS

The Advanced modules ☐

Opportunities to sail regularly ☐

Introduction to high-performance boats ☐

Local club racing ☐

Chief Instructor's/Principal's Signature

RYA Training Centre

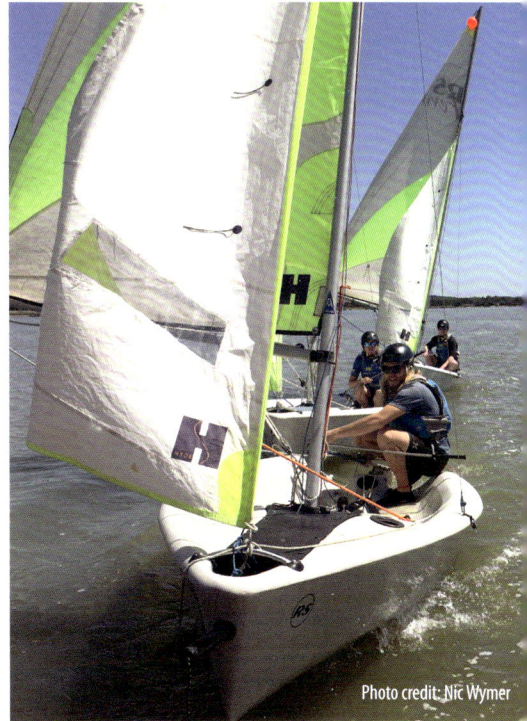
Photo credit: Nic Wymer

SEAMANSHIP SKILLS

On successful completion of this course, you will be capable of manoeuvring a dinghy/keelboat/multihull in a seamanlike manner and making seamanship decisions in moderate conditions.

It will be assumed that, when starting on this course, you have already mastered the practical skills and absorbed the background knowledge required for the previous levels.

Tuition will be given by trained Instructors, using appropriate supervision ratios with regard to the location and competence of the students. Much of the work afloat will be done without an Instructor aboard. The emphasis is on increasing the self-reliance and decision-making of the sailor.

Duration: Approximately 16 hours (either spread over a series of sessions or two full days).

Practical

ROPEWORK

Can tie a fisherman's bend, rolling hitch, and sheet bend ☐

LAUNCHING AND RECOVERY

Can leave and return to beach, jetty, or mooring, including windward and leeward shore ☐

Sailing techniques and manoeuvres ☐

Can:

Heave to ☐

Reef afloat ☐

Recover a man overboard ☐

Be towed by a power-driven vessel ☐

Anchor, including understanding principles and techniques for different circumstances† ☐

Sail backwards ☐

Sail in adverse circumstances (no rudder, no centreboard)*† ☐

Prepare a road trailer and secure a boat for transportation (optional) ☐

Sailing Background

SAILING THEORY AND BACKGROUND

Understands the following terminology:

Windward, leeward, abeam, forward, aft, ahead, astern, to weather, downwind, amidships, quarter, pinching, sailing by the lee, luff, bear away, planing, sternway, broaching ☐

Knows and can apply the following International Regulations for the Prevention of Collisions at Sea (IRPCS):

Meeting other sailing vessels, meeting power-driven vessels, following or crossing narrow channels, action by stand-on vessel ☐

CAPSIZE RECOVERY

Knows how to recover from total inversion (practical session if possible) ☐

*Not necessarily applicable to keelboats
†Not necessarily applicable to multihulls

METEOROLOGY

Knows sources of information on weather patterns for the day ☐

Can interpret forecasts and understand local effects ☐

Is aware of Beaufort Wind Scale and changing weather conditions, including fog ☐

Can use local tide tables ☐

Understands rate of rise and fall – Twelfths Rule ☐

Is aware of tidal streams ☐

Has a basic understanding of charts and important symbols ☐

Experienced Sailor's Direct Assessment

The candidate should be able to demonstrate satisfactorily aspects of practical and theory knowledge, afloat and ashore, answering any questions. ☐

_____

Chief Instructor's/Principal's Signature

_____

RYA Training Centre

Photo credit: Nic Wymer

DAY SAILING

The course will include the planning and execution of a day sail, and, on successful completion, you will have a confident, safe approach to planning and executing a short day sail in a dinghy/keelboat/multihull.

On starting this course you should have already mastered the practical skills and absorbed the background knowledge required for the previous levels. In addition, sailors wishing to cruise independently should ensure that they understand and can carry out the manoeuvres in the Seamanship Skills (see page 16) part of the RYA National Sailing Scheme.

Candidates who hold the RYA Essential Navigation and Seamanship course completion certificate or a higher-level RYA cruising award may gain exemption from necessary chartwork.

Duration: Approximately 16 hours (either spread over a series of sessions or two full days).

Photo credit: Nic Wymer

Practical

RIGGING

Can prepare and equip a boat for cruising, including safety and navigation equipment, clothing and food, and stow gear correctly ☐

SAILING TECHNIQUES AND MANOEUVRES

Can plan and undertake a day sail including a consideration of pilotage/navigation and collision avoidance ☐

Can use the anchor to effect lee-shore landing and departure*† ☐

ADVERSE CONDITIONS

Is able to self-rescue following total inversion* ☐

Understands how to improvise in the event of gear failure ☐

Sailing Background

SAILING THEORY AND BACKGROUND

Has knowledge of boat handling in strong winds and difficult conditions (practical where possible) ☐

NAVIGATION

Can plan a day's cruise in coastal waters, including knowledge of:

Publications available, particularly charts, tide tables, tidal stream atlases ☐

Navigational instruments and their limitations afloat ☐

Use of GPS, including waypoint navigation ☐

Confirming position by another source ☐

Tidal heights and tidal streams (Rule of Twelfths or percentage rule), probable changes in the weather, and the interaction of weather and tidal streams ☐

Decision-making in adverse circumstances, including planning alternatives and refuges ☐

Magnetic compass: variation and deviation ☐

Interpretation of charts ☐

Use of transits and bearings to steer course and fix position ☐

Recording position and principles of dead reckoning ☐

METEOROLOGY

Knows sources of information on weather patterns for the day ☐

Understands main characteristics of high- and low-pressure systems and simple interpretation of synoptic charts ☐

Has awareness of changing weather conditions ☐

Experienced Sailor's Direct Assessment

The candidate should be able to demonstrate satisfactorily competence in areas of both practical and background knowledge, ashore and afloat. ☐

Chief Instructor's/Principal's Signature

RYA Training Centre

*Not necessarily applicable to keelboats
†Not necessarily applicable to multihulls

Photo credit: Nic Wymer

SAILING WITH SPINNAKERS

On successful completion of this course you will understand how to sail a dinghy/keelboat/multihull rigged with an asymmetric or symmetric spinnaker. It is assumed when starting this course you have already mastered the practical skills and absorbed the background knowledge required for previous levels. Tuition will be given by an Advanced Instructor, or by an Instructor with appropriate experience approved by the Principal, using appropriate supervision ratios with regard to the location and competence of the students.

Duration: Approximately 16 hours (either spread over a series of sessions or two full days).

Photo credit: Nic Wymer

Photo credit: Paul Wyeth

Practical

RIGGING

Can rig boats, including spinnaker, and trapeze where fitted ☐

LAUNCHING AND RECOVERY

Understands how to launch boats with open transoms and/or racks*† ☐

SAILING TECHNIQUES AND MANOEUVRES

Can sail as crew or helm using equipment to good advantage ☐

Can perform spinnaker hoist, gybe, and drop as crew or helm ☐

Understands and can sail best course downwind ☐

CAPSIZE RECOVERY

Can perform capsize recovery including spinnaker ☐

Knows how to recover from total inversion* ☐

Sailing Background

RACING

Has knowledge of courses for type of boat ☐

SAILING THEORY AND BACKGROUND

Understands the concept of apparent wind sailing ☐

Understands the effect of hull shape on performance ☐

Can access sources of information and apply rig setup for different conditions ☐

Experienced Sailor's Direct Assessment

Candidates should be able to demonstrate satisfactorily competence and confidence in areas afloat and ashore, practical and of sailing background. ☐

Chief Instructor's/Principal's Signature

RYA Training Centre

*Not necessarily applicable to keelboats
†Not necessarily applicable to multihulls

PERFORMANCE SAILING

On successful completion of this course, you will understand how to sail performance dinghies/keelboats/multihulls in all wind conditions that you can expect to encounter, sailing the boat to best advantage at all times.

The emphasis is on coaching to improve your sailing performance and will therefore involve coaching from powerboats. This course is intended primarily for two-person spinnaker boats; however, it may be delivered in performance single-handers and the certificate endorsed accordingly.

Tuition will be given by an Advanced Instructor for the type of boat, using appropriate supervision ratios with regard to the location and competence of the students, and the need to provide continuous feedback on the water. It is assumed that every student starting this course has already mastered the practical skills and absorbed the background knowledge required for previous levels. In practical terms, at least a full season's sailing experience since learning to sail is advisable.

Duration: Approximately 16 hours (either spread over a series of sessions or two full days).

Photo credit: Nic Wymer

Practical

RIGGING

Can rig any type of boat, including spinnaker and trapeze (if fitted) ☐

Understands basic rig setup and tuning ☐

SAILING TECHNIQUES AND MANOEUVRES

Can make best possible use of crew and equipment to sail efficiently on all points of sailing in a variety of conditions, including symmetric or asymmetric spinnaker ☐

Can use sail controls to effect changes to shape and power of sails ☐

Can spot and use wind shifts and gusts to effect best course up and down wind ☐

Can perform capsize recovery including spinnaker. Knows how to recover from total inversion* ☐

Can tack, refining skills according to conditions ☐

Shows understanding of roll-tacking principles ☐

Can gybe, refining skills according to conditions ☐

Shows understanding of roll-gybing principles ☐

Sailing Background

SAILING THEORY AND BACKGROUND

Understands how to make use of wind variation and tidal eddies which occur due to geographical features and tidal conditions ☐

Has an understanding of hull shapes and rig types, including their effect on performance ☐

Understands planing and the effect of rails ☐

*Not necessarily applicable to keelboats

METEOROLOGY

Knows sources of information on weather patterns for the day ☐

Understands main characteristics of high- and low-pressure systems, and simple interpretation of synoptic charts ☐

Has awareness of changing weather conditions ☐

Experienced Sailor's Direct Assessment

Candidates should show confidence and competence in practical and sailing background areas, both afloat and ashore. ☐

_____

Chief Instructor's/Principal's Signature

_____

RYA Training Centre

Photo credit: Nic Wymer

23

RYA SAILFOILING COURSES: FIRST FLIGHTS

This first session in SAILfoiling provides an initial introduction into the amazing and exhilarating world of foiling. As a pre-requisite, you should hold the RYA Level 2 Basic Skills, which will ensure you have the necessary skills to take on foiling!

Aimed as a taster session, First Flights provides you with a basic introduction to foiling, assisting you to make your first foiling take-offs.

Suggested course length: Two to four hours (taster session).

Practical

RIGGING

Has knowledge of:

Assembling and setting up the main foil, rudder, and rudder foil ☐

Various foiling boats ☐

The options and adaptions available for non-foiling boats ☐

Launching and Recovery

Has knowledge of the different launch/recovery methods for different boat designs ☐

SAILING TECHNIQUES AND MANOEUVRES

Can:

Engage and disengage foils ☐

Change course sailed, and adjust sail trim to encourage flight ☐

Take off ☐

Understands and has knowledge of:

How to land safely ☐

How to maintain foiling ☐

Capsize recovery methods ☐

Apparent wind, showing a basic application and sail adjustment ☐

FOILING KNOWLEDGE

Understands and has knowledge of:

The basic theory of how foils work ☐

A range of different foiling boats ☐

Sail adjustments, and how to trim sails ☐

SAFETY

Understands and has knowledge of:

The risks of foiling alone ☐

The lack of noise when approaching other craft ☐

Different personal safety equipment ☐

The importance of foiling in suitable sailing conditions ☐

Chief Instructor's/Principal's Signature

RYA Training Centre

SUSTAINED FLIGHTS

Sustained Flights is designed to increase your foil handling and control. Having completed this course, you will start to feel more confident about the practical techniques and theory required to foil, steer, and maintain a course effectively. All tacking or gybing at this level is non-foiling.

It will be assumed that every student starting this course has already mastered the practical skills and absorbed the background knowledge required for First Flights.

Suggested course length: Up to 16 hours, either spread over a series of sessions or full days.

Photo credit: Ian Aldridge (Minorca Sailing)

Practical

RIGGING

Can assemble and set up the main foil (with assistance) ☐

Can assemble and set up the rudder and rudder foil (with assistance) ☐

Has knowledge of how to adjust foils in different conditions to optimise performance ☐

Understands how to trim the main foil to adjust the 'ride height' ☐

LAUNCHING AND RECOVERY

Can:

Launch the boat off a slipway/beach using a method specific for that foiling boat (with assistance) ☐

Safely return to slipway/beach using a method specific to that foiling boat ☐

SAILING TECHNIQUE AND MANOEUVRES

Can:

Maintain periods of sustained foiling ☐

Trim sails effectively according to the apparent wind ☐

Demonstrate a non-foiling tack ☐

Demonstrate a non-foiling gybe ☐

Adjust bow height and trim through the rudder foil ☐

Show basic skills and understanding of foiling on various points of sail ☐

FOILING KNOWLEDGE

Technique:

Understands the apparent-wind effect and how to trim effectively according to the point of sail ☐

Understands different ride heights and how to adjust the main foil to enable the boat to ride higher or lower ☐

Has knowledge of correct angles for tack entry and exit ☐

Has knowledge of correct angles for gybe entry and exit ☐

Theory

Understands:

How the wand works ☐

How twist tillers adjust the rudder ☐

Righting moment and how it is achieved ☐

SAFETY

Has knowledge of safety equipment which may be worn while foiling ☐

_____

Chief Instructor's/Principal's Signature

_____

RYA Training Centre

Photo credit: Paul Wyeth

PERFORMANCE FLIGHTS

Performance Flights is the last of the RYA foiling courses, looking at advanced skills and technique. This course will increase your confidence on different angles, while also looking at entry and exit into manoeuvres, providing you with a good understanding as to the theory.

It will be assumed that every student starting this course has the knowledge and practical ability of RYA Sustained Flights or above.

Suggested course length: Up to 16 hours, either spread over a series of sessions or full days.

Practical

SAILING TECHNIQUE AND MANOEUVRES

Can:

Demonstrate foiling upwind and downwind ☐

Effectively set up, balance, and steer into the tack ☐

Demonstrate tack entry while foiling, exiting in control ☐

Can:

Effectively set up, balance, and steer into the gybe ☐

Demonstrate gybe entry while foiling, exiting in control ☐

FOILING KNOWLEDGE

Can:

Steer and adopt the correct body movements required to foil through a gybe ☐

Adjust wand settings and ride height for optimum performance in different conditions ☐

Understands:

The theory and technique required to set up and approach the 'entry' of a foiling tack and gybe ☐

The theory and technique required to set up and approach the 'exit' for a foiling tack and gybe ☐

What causes and how to deal with a pitch pole (specific boats) ☐

Different wand systems and what they are used for ☐

SAFETY

Understands the importance of safe sailing areas and suitable sailing conditions to assist with the practise of performance-foiling manoeuvres ☐

Chief Instructor's/Principal's Signature

RYA Training Centre

Photo credit: Paul Wyeth

RYA RACING COURSES: START RACING

The first course in the racing syllabus, Start Racing, will develop and provide you with the basic skills needed to enter a race and understand the simple techniques, sequences, and rules. To take this course every student should have mastered the practical skills to Level 2/Stage 3 or above. This course is delivered by a Recognised Training Centre.

Suggested course length: 16 hours.

Photo credit: Nic Wymer

STARTS

Understands a basic start sequence ☐

Can identify a start line and start from the correct side ☐

Can slow the boat and accelerate to cross the line within 10 seconds after the start signal ☐

Understands the procedure if over the line at the start ☐

Understands the significance of port/starboard and windward/leeward ☐

BOAT HANDLING

Can tack and gybe in a range of conditions ☐

Understands the use of heel and trim to aid steering ☐

Understands an appropriate technique to approach and land when coming ashore, on lee shores, weather shores, or slipways ☐

Can recover from a capsize with little assistance ☐

Can perform an MOB recovery to Level 2 standard ☐

SPEED

Can use the five essentials effectively ☐

Can keep the boat upright using the toe straps to sit out and can trim the sail to aid this ☐

Can hold an effective close-hauled course upwind ☐

TACTICS

Understands how to round a mark ☐

Can recognise headers and lift ☐

Has knowledge of the difference between the International Regulations for Preventing Collisions at Sea (IRPCS) and the Racing Rules of Sailing (RRS). Understands other rules as shown ☐

STRATEGY

Can source and use an appropriate weather forecast ☐

Understands what a suitable wind strength is to race in ☐

Experienced Sailor's Direct Assessment

The candidate should be able to demonstrate satisfactorily aspects of practical and theory knowledge, afloat and ashore, answering any questions. ☐

_____

Instructor's/Racing Coach's signature

_____

RYA Training Centre

Photo credit: Paddy James (RS Sailing)

CLUB RACING

The Club Racing course has been designed to improve boat handling and speed, while providing an understanding of developing a strategic plan based on the conditions. Students taking this course should have the minimum knowledge of Start Racing. This course can be delivered by a Race Coach Level 2 or 3 within either a Recognised Training Centre or an affiliated club.

STARTS

Understands line bias and can identify the biased end ☐

Has knowledge of how the fleet of boats may impact on the start strategy ☐

Understands how the strategy for the first beat may impact the starting position ☐

Can successfully start on their home club line (for sailors completing the course at their home club) ☐

BOAT HANDLING

Can slow the boat effectively and accelerate ☐

Can use heel to help the boat tack and gybe ☐

If appropriate, can hoist, gybe, fly, and drop a spinnaker ☐

Can demonstrate the importance of good communication and teamwork for effective racing ☐

SPEED

Can adapt the rig to different conditions ☐

Can use a tuning guide appropriate to the boat being used ☐

Keelboats: understands how to use the backstay to control mast bend ☐

Multihulls: understands how to depower the rig in strong wind conditions ☐

TACTICS

Understands the significance of laylines and how to judge them when afloat ☐

Understands the importance of clean air ☐

Understands tactics within a handicap fleet (if appropriate) ☐

Can demonstrate application of Section A and Section B of the Racing Rules of Sailing (RRS) ☐

Understands how the rules apply at marks and obstructions (Section C of the RRS) ☐

STRATEGY

Understands the effect of water current on the boat and how the topography (buildings, trees, hills) can affect the wind over a course ☐

Can use a suitable weather app to give an indication of wind trend over the period of a race and how to use that to best effect ☐

Can occasionally demonstrate the ability to tack or gybe on wind shifts ☐

Instructor's/Racing Coach's signature

RYA Training Centre

Photo credit: Paddy James (RS Sailing)

REGIONAL RACING

Learn and develop skills which will enhance your ability to adapt to the changing conditions and different venues, as well as the skills needed to respond. Regional Racing will also provide the skills and techniques needed to analyse effectively post-race. This course can be delivered by a Race Coach Level 2 or 3 within either a Recognised Training Centre or an affiliated club.

Photo Credit: Paddy James (RS Sailing)

STARTS

Can create and protect a space to leeward ☐

Can demonstrate starting from different parts of the start line ☐

Can formulate and execute a pre-start plan ☐

Can demonstrate a practical understanding of the signals explained in Part 3 of the Racing Rules of Sailing (RRS) ☐

BOAT HANDLING

Can adapt to different types of boat ☐

Understands the different techniques used for a range of different craft ☐

Can demonstrate all previous learning over a wide range of wind conditions where possible ☐

SPEED

Understands the differences between stayed rigs and unstayed rigs ☐

Can alter the rig while racing to suit conditions where possible ☐

Understands how to record settings and duplicate them ☐

TACTICS

Can identify the layline for a mark and allow for the conditions and the effect of the fleet ☐

Understands the importance of when to sail the fleet and when to engage with another boat ☐

Can demonstrate both a tight and loose cover on another boat ☐

Has knowledge of how to use a compass
to best effect ☐

Understands all of Part 2 of the Racing Rules
of Sailing (RRS) and can demonstrate taking
a penalty effectively ☐

Understands the process for raising a protest and
actions when being protested ☐

STRATEGY

Can develop a strategy that accounts for the weather
conditions expected, the tide/current expected, and
the type of fleet. This should be discussed with the
coach/instructor prior to the race and will be seen
to be executed ☐

Instructor's/Racing Coach's signature

RYA Training Centre

Photo credit: James Tomlinson

CHAMPIONSHIP RACING

This is more personalised training than a course, and requires a less syllabus-based approach, taking into consideration the needs of the sailor and varying the areas covered accordingly. It is quite likely to be the end result of a full training programme. Championship Racing is delivered by an RYA Race Coach Level 3 within a Recognised Training Centre or an affiliated club, over a minimum of 50 hours (25 hours on the water).

STARTS

Can take the strategy and adopt the most applicable start ☐

Can recover and adapt the start where appropriate ☐

Can demonstrate recovering from a start which has not gone to plan ☐

BOAT HANDLING

Can demonstrate a high level of boat handling in all conditions and is able to adapt the techniques used to suit conditions ☐

Can use analysis to develop improved techniques ☐

SPEED

Understands how to keep records of the settings and to develop them to suit the conditions/sailors ☐

Understands how to use a tuning partner, video, and post-race analysis to refine further the tuning guide and techniques employed ☐

Can develop and demonstrate how to sail in different conditions ☐

TACTICS

Understands all the relevant racing rules and how to use them to best effect for the outcome of the race ☐

Understands how to analyse a series of races and to implement strategies to secure the best outcome ☐

Understands when to race conservatively and when to race aggressively and can demonstrate these ☐

Can demonstrate use of 'boat-on-boat' and 'boat-on-fleet' tactics during racing/training ☐

STRATEGY

Can develop, plan, and adapt the strategy to take into account the unfolding landscape of a race while still showing consistent boat speed ☐

Level 3 Racing Coach's signature

RYA Training Centre

Photo credit: Nick Dempsey

Instructor Training

If you have enjoyed your experiences of learning to sail and developing your sailing techniques and skills through the RYA National Sailing Scheme, why not consider sharing your enthusiasm, expertise, and skills with others by becoming involved in the RYA Instructor Training programme?

Below are brief details concerning the basic training courses. More information can be found in G14 RYA National Sailing Scheme Instructor Handbook.

RYA ASSISTANT INSTRUCTOR

Duration: Two days/20 hours

The RYA Assistant Instructor is trained to assist qualified Instructors to teach beginners up to the standard of the RYA National Sailing Scheme Level 2 and the RYA Youth Sailing Scheme Stage 3. They must only work under the supervision of a Senior Instructor. The award is centre-specific.

ELIGIBILITY FOR THE TRAINING COURSE

Pass one of the RYA National Sailing Scheme Advanced Modules or equivalent personal sailing standard. Recommendation by Principal of training centre.

TRAINING

Training will cover the centre's safe-operation procedures and the teaching points related to teaching beginners. The award is centre-specific.

Training is based on a two-day or modular course of 20 hours' duration at the centre run by the Principal/Chief Instructor who holds a valid RYA Senior Instructor certificate.

ASSESSMENT

Candidates will be assessed on their practical teaching ability with beginners. Successful candidates will be awarded an RYA Assistant Instructor certificate by their Principal.

RYA Instructor Pre-entry Sailing Assessment

The Pre-entry is an essential prerequisite to the RYA Dinghy Instructor course. It is a practical test determining whether a candidate has the required sailing ability, control, and seamanship to become an Instructor. The assessment is conducted by an RYA Trainer and only valid for one year. During the assessment candidates are judged on their preparation and execution of each task, including awareness of others, and showing confident sailing at all times with awareness of 'the Five Essentials'. During the assessment, the Trainer will be seeking to confirm the candidate can sail in a controlled and competent manner, considering preparation, communication, approach, and execution for each exercise. These may include: sail around a triangular course; sail a tight circular course; sail a follow-my-leader course; pick up a man-overboard dummy, and other skills-based exercises including rudderless, lee-shore landing and departure, pick up mooring or anchor, come alongside a moored boat, and recover a capsized dinghy and sail away. This provides an overall impression of sailing ability and whether it is of the standard required to attend the instructor course.

DINGHY/KEELBOAT/MULTIHULL/ FOILING INSTRUCTOR

Duration: Five days/50 hours.

It is possible to complete the RYA National Sailing Scheme in dinghies, keelboats, or multihulls. Therefore, Instructors teaching the Scheme must be qualified for the type of boat in which they will be teaching. The Instructor certificate will show whether the Instructor is qualified to teach on inland or coastal waters (depending on where they completed the pre-entry sailing assessment and course).

ROLE

Competent, experienced sailor able to sail in strong winds

Can teach RYA National Sailing Scheme up to and including Seamanship Skills, Day Sailing, Sailing with Spinnakers, and RYA Youth Sailing Scheme Stages 1–4

Will only work under the supervision of the RYA Senior Instructor

ELIGIBILITY FOR THE TRAINING COURSE

Minimum age 16

Valid first aid certificate
(see www.rya.org.uk/go/firstaid)

RYA Powerboat Level 2 certificate

RYA Safe & Fun

Pre-entry sailing assessment completed

RYA membership

TRAINING

- The structure and content of the RYA National Sailing Scheme and RYA Youth Sailing Scheme
- Training in RYA teaching methods, including teaching both adults and children
- Preparation and presentation of a lesson
- Preparation and use of visual aids
- The assessment of students' abilities
- The use of powered craft in a teaching environment

ASSESSMENT

The assessment will be based on an overall (or holistic) judgement throughout the week and during the Instructor moderation day.

This assessment will include:

- Enthusiasm for the sport
- Sailing ability
- Confidence and knowledge in the subject
- Awareness of safety
- Practical teaching according to RYA methods
- Theory knowledge
- Successful demonstrations and clear explanations
- Correct diagnosis and tactful correction of students' faults
- Safe powerboat handling in a teaching environment

Photo credit: Nic Wymer

PERSONAL LOG

| DATE | TYPE OF BOAT | HOURS' EXPERIENCE | | ACTIVITY & WEATHER CONDITIONS | | AUTHORISATION |
		HELM	CREW	TYPE OF COURSE OR ACTIVITY	MAX WIND SPEED	CENTRE/CLUB INSTRUCTOR

PERSONAL LOG

DATE	TYPE OF BOAT	HOURS' EXPERIENCE		ACTIVITY & WEATHER CONDITIONS		AUTHORISATION
		HELM	CREW	TYPE OF COURSE OR ACTIVITY	MAX WIND SPEED	CENTRE/CLUB INSTRUCTOR

COURSE CERTIFICATES

COURSE CERTIFICATES

PLEASE ATTACH YOUR
RYA CERTIFICATE HERE

Please note that no record of
certificates is held by the RYA

Enquiries about lost certificates
should be made to the centre
where the course was taken

RYA

COURSE CERTIFICATES

RYA

COURSE CERTIFICATES

**PLEASE ATTACH YOUR
RYA CERTIFICATE HERE**

Please note that no record of
certificates is held by the RYA

Enquiries about lost certificates
should be made to the centre
where the course was taken

COURSE CERTIFICATES

COURSE CERTIFICATES

Please note that no record of certificates is held by the RYA

Enquiries about lost certificates should be made to the centre where the course was taken

COURSE CERTIFICATES

COURSE CERTIFICATES

Please note that no record of
certificates is held by the RYA

Enquiries about lost certificates
should be made to the centre
where the course was taken

COURSE CERTIFICATES

RYA

COURSE CERTIFICATES

**PLEASE ATTACH YOUR
RYA CERTIFICATE HERE**

Please note that no record of
certificates is held by the RYA

Enquiries about lost certificates
should be made to the centre
where the course was taken

RYA

COURSE CERTIFICATES

COURSE CERTIFICATES

Please note that no record of
certificates is held by the RYA

Enquiries about lost certificates
should be made to the centre
where the course was taken

COURSE CERTIFICATES

COURSE CERTIFICATES

Please note that no record of
certificates is held by the RYA

Enquiries about lost certificates
should be made to the centre
where the course was taken

RYA